TUSKEGEE AIRMEN QUESTIONS AND ANSWERS FOR STUDENTS AND TEACHERS

Tuskegee Airmen Questions and Answers for Students and Teachers

Daniel Haulman

NewSouth Books

Montgomery

NewSouth Books
105 S. Court Street
Montgomery, AL 36104

Copyright © 2015 by Daniel Haulman
All rights reserved under International and Pan-American Copyright Conventions.
Published in the United States by NewSouth Books, a division of NewSouth, Inc.,
Montgomery, Alabama.

Publisher's Cataloging-in-Publication data

Haulman, Daniel
Tuskegee Airmen questions and answers for students and teachers / Daniel Haulman
p. cm.

ISBN 978-1-60306-381-4 (paperback)
ISBN 978-1-60306-382-1 (ebook)

1. United States. Army Air Forces—African American troops. 2. African American
pilots—History—20th century. 3. World War, 1939–1945—Participation, African
American. 4. World War, 1939–1945—Aerial operations, American. I. Title.

2014960106

Printed in the United States of America

To the memory of my father,
Clement R. Haulman,
a B-24 bomber pilot during World War II

Contents

Introduction

The history of the Tuskegee Airmen well deserves the perennial attention it generates. As a historian at the Air Force Historical Research Agency at Maxwell Air Force Base, I have had the opportunity to respond to a host of questions about the first African American pilots in American military history, whose performance in World War II refuted the racist stereotypes of the past by demonstrating that black men could fly in combat as well as anyone. While flying bomber escort missions, they lost fewer B-17and B-24 heavy bombers to enemy aircraft than the average of the other fighter groups in the Fifteenth Air Force. The Tuskegee Airmen shot down 112 enemy airplanes and earned 96 Distinguished Flying Crosses. Their units earned three Distinguished Unit Citations. Their heroic exploits have become legendary but have also generated some misconceptions that need correction.

The fact that the Air Force Historical Research Agency is one of the best repositories of historical information about the Tuskegee Airmen gives me the resources I need to answer most questions about the Tuskegee Airmen record. Since 2006, I have attended seven Tuskegee Airmen Incorporated national conventions, and those meetings have also generated many inquiries about the true achievements of the Tuskegee Airmen. I have also spoken at a great many libraries and other venues about Tuskegee Airmen publications that I have authored or co-authored, and those talks have also stimulated a great many questions about the Tuskegee Airmen. Over the years, I began to notice that most of the inquiries were ones I had heard before. To answer them for more people than I could hope to meet personally, I have collected the most common questions about the Tuskegee Airmen and answered them in this publication.

I think this collection of questions about the Tuskegee Airmen and the correct answers will be especially useful in schools, because of the large number of students interested in the topic. To make examination of the subject more logical, I have arranged the questions in a chronological format.

Questions about training, for example, generally precede those about combat operations, and questions about the fighter group and its squadrons precede those regarding the bombardment group and its squadrons.

I think any student who becomes familiar with these questions and answers would have a good understanding of what the Tuskegee Airmen did and did not do, when they did what they did, where they were stationed, who the leaders were, and even why and how their units came into existence.

I have not neglected the pioneering consequences of the Airmen's combat record. They truly demonstrated that African Americans could fly successfully in combat, refuting the old myth of inferiority, and paving the way for future opportunities for others of their race.

Thus anyone who seeks a short history of the Tuskegee Airmen can get it by reading the brief answers that follow, while ignoring the questions. Reading both, however, is useful especially for students who are studying the record of these African Americans in the Army Air Forces and preparing for possible test questions.

The questions, on the other hand, may be especially useful for teachers of the subject, especially during February's Black History Month. Anyone wishing to refresh his or her own knowledge of Tuskegee Airmen history need only attempt to answer the questions without help, with the accurate answers readily available.

Having taught high school social studies for five years myself, and also ten college courses at various colleges and universities in the Montgomery area over the years, I am familiar with the curiosity of students, especially about heroic figures with whom they might identify, and the thirst for knowledge which this small book might help satisfy.

Frequently Asked Questions

1. Who were the Tuskegee Airmen?

The Tuskegee Airmen were the first black pilots in American military history, and those who were stationed at the bases where they trained or from which they flew, and those who belonged to the organizations to which the pilots belonged, or to the support organizations for those flying units. The pilots were called Tuskegee Airmen because they trained at airfields around Tuskegee during World War II. The Tuskegee Airmen Incorporated uses the term DOTA (Documented Original Tuskegee Airman) to define anyone, "man or woman, military or civilian, black or white, officer or enlisted," who served at any of the air bases at which the Tuskegee-trained pilots trained or flew, or any of the Army Air Force units "stemming from the 'Tuskegee Experience' between the years 1941 and 1949."

2. How did the first black pilots in the US military get started?

When he was running for a third term as President, in 1940, Franklin D. Roosevelt promised to allow blacks to become military pilots. The War Department agreed to do that, but with the understanding that the black military pilots would be trained on a segregated basis, and serve in their own segregated units.

3. What was the first black flying unit in the US military?

The first black flying unit in history was the 99th Pursuit Squadron, which was redesignated later as the 99th Fighter Squadron. It was first activated at Chanute Field, Illinois, in March 1941, but it did not at first have any pilots assigned, because they had not yet been trained.

4. Why was Tuskegee chosen as the place for black military pilot training?

Tuskegee was chosen as the place for the first black military pilot training because Tuskegee Institute had already been training black civilian pilots, the climate was better than the North for flying, Tuskegee Institute lobbied for the contract for the primary flight school, and the area already had a segregated environment, which was consistent with the segregated training.

5.   When did the first black military pilots graduate?

The first black military pilots graduated in March of 1942. Although 13 started the training, only five completed it. One of the five was Benjamin O. Davis, Jr., a West Point graduate whose father was the first black general in the U.S. Army. There were black pilots before March 1942, but not in the armed services of the United States.

6.   Who were some of the leaders of black pilot training at Tuskegee?

One of the black flight instructors of the primary flight training phase at Moton Field was Charles Alfred Anderson, whom the students called "Chief" because he had been the chief civilian pilot instructor at Kennedy Field before that. One of the most important white flight instructors at Tuskegee Army Air Field, who taught advanced flying training to single engine pilots, was Major Robert Long. The commander of the flight training school at Tuskegee Army Air Field was Col. Noel Parrish. The cadets admired the training they received from Anderson, Long, and Parrish, and remembered them as being fair in their treatment.

7.   What were the phases of military flying training?

Before flying aircraft, black military pilot cadets underwent pre-flight training. Most of the Tuskegee Airmen received this training at Tuskegee Institute. After that, there were three phases of military flying training, that most cadets had to complete before receiving their wings as Army Air Forces pilots: primary, basic, and advanced. The graduates then proceeded to transition training, to learn how to fly specific warplanes before entering combat. Those warplanes included fighters or bombers. Liaison and service pilots had fewer flight training phases.

8. What are the definitions of liaison pilot and service pilot?

A liaison pilot was one trained to fly light aircraft in a battlefield area for such tasks as artillery spotting. A service pilot was one trained to fly aircraft other than those used in combat.

9. Where did the black military pilot training take place?

The primary phase took place at Moton Field, much of which (35 acres) is now the Tuskegee Airmen National Historic Site. The basic, advanced, and original transition flying training phases took place at a much larger airfield called Tuskegee Army Air Field, several miles to the northwest of Moton Field, and today in ruins in the country between Tuskegee and Tallassee. Additional transition training took place in the 553nd Fighter Squadron at Selfridge Field, Michigan, and later at Walterboro Army Air Field, South Carolina.

10. What kinds of airplanes did the Tuskegee Airmen fly in training?

In primary flying training, the Tuskegee Airmen flew PT-17 and PT-13 biplanes, and occasionally P-19 monoplanes, on a grass strip at Moton Field. In basic flying training at Tuskegee Army Air Field, they flew BT-13 airplanes, and later AT-6s. In advanced flying training, also at Tuskegee Army Air Field, future fighter pilots flew AT-6 airplanes, and future bomber pilots flew twin-engine AT-10 airplanes. Later, the AT-10 planes were replaced by TB-25s. For transition training the future fighter pilots flew P-40s and the future bomber pilots flew B-25s. Fighter pilots also flew P-39s and P-47s in transition training beyond Tuskegee.

11. How many classes of pilots graduated from advanced pilot training at Tuskegee Army Air Field?

There were 44 classes of pilots who graduated from advanced flying training at Tuskegee Army Air Field.

12. How many black Tuskegee Airmen pilots were there in all?

There were 930 pilots who graduated from advanced flying training at

Class 44A of Tuskegee Airmen pilots, who graduated at Tuskegee Army Air Field on 7 January 1944.

Tuskegee Army Air Field. In addition to that, there were 51 liaison pilots who trained there, and 11 service pilots, for a total of 992 black pilots who were Tuskegee Airmen pilots. There were also a few black liaison pilots, but only a handful, who graduated from liaison pilot training at Fort Sill instead of from pilot training at Tuskegee Army Air Field. If one counts Ernest J. Davis, Jr., who completed primary flight training at Moton Field in Tuskegee but his basic and advanced flying training at Stewart Field in New York (because he was a West Point cadet), the total number of Tuskegee Airmen pilots would be 993.

13. Were there any black pilots who graduated from advanced flying training at Tuskegee Army Air Field who were from foreign countries?

Five Haitian pilots graduated from advanced pilot training at Tuskegee Army Air Field.

14. How many Tuskegee Airmen were there, if you count not

only the pilots but all navigators, bombardiers, armorers, maintainers, trainers, administrators, and support personnel?

Counting all the Tuskegee Airmen, there were more than 14,000.

15. Which of the Tuskegee Airmen flying organizations took part in combat overseas?

The 332nd Fighter Group and the 99th, 100th, 301st, and 302nd Fighter Squadrons took part in combat overseas. There were other Tuskegee Airmen organizations overseas that provided support for the flying organizations, but their personnel did not fly aircraft in combat.

16. When did the 99th Fighter Squadron first go overseas?

The 99th Fighter Squadron deployed to North Africa during April 1943, a little more than a year after its first pilots graduated from advanced flying training, and more than two years after the squadron was first activated. Within the next few months, the squadron moved from North Africa to Sicily and then to the mainland of Italy.

17. When did the 99th Fighter Squadron fly its first combat mission?

The 99th Fighter Squadron flew its first combat mission on 2 Jun 1943, more than a month after it arrived in North Africa.

18. When did a 99th Fighter Squadron pilot first shoot down an enemy airplane?

1st Lt. Charles B. Hall scored the first 99th Fighter Squadron aerial victory credit on 2 Jul 1943, a month after the squadron entered combat.

19. Did the 99th Fighter Squadron face opposition from white officers overseas?

Yes. For example, Col. William W. Momyer, commander of the white 33rd Fighter Group, to which the 99th Fighter Squadron was attached, tried to have the 99th Fighter Squadron taken out of combat, claiming that it was performing poorly. His recommendation was supported by his immediate superiors. The War Department undertook a study to compare the combat performance of the 99th Fighter Squadron with the other P-40 fighter squadrons in the Mediterranean Theater of Operations, but found no significant difference. The 99th Fighter Squadron was attached to other white fighter groups after the complaint was sent.

20. What kinds of airplanes did the Tuskegee Airmen first fly in combat?

The 99th Fighter Squadron first flew P-40 Warhawk airplanes in combat. They were the same type of airplane the "Flying Tigers" had flown in Asia. The 99th Fighter Squadron was one of many fighter squadrons in the Twelfth Air Force at the time that also flew P-40 airplanes, and was not flying inferior airplanes to the ones the white pilots were flying in the groups to which the 99th Fighter Squadron was attached.

21. Was the 99th Fighter Squadron successful overseas?

Yes. The 99th Fighter Squadron distinguished itself in missions over Anzio, Italy, in January 1944. In two days of intense operations, it shot down more enemy airplanes than the other P-40 squadrons in the area. The 99th Fighter Squadron also shot down a great many other airplanes on other days.

22. What was the first black flying group, and when was it first activated?

The first black flying group was the 332nd Fighter Group, and it was first activated at Tuskegee Army Air Field on 13 October 1942.

23. What squadrons belonged to the 332nd Fighter Group?

The 332nd Fighter Group at first included the 100th, 301st, and 302nd Fighter Squadrons. At first the 99th Fighter Squadron did not belong to it. When the 99th Fighter Squadron deployed overseas, the 332nd Fighter Group stayed stateside.

24. Where did the 332nd Fighter Group move after Tuskegee?

In late March, 1943, the 332nd Fighter Group moved from Tuskegee

Army Air Field in Alabama to Selfridge Field, Michigan, to continue training after its pilots graduated from advanced flight training at Tuskegee.
Selfridge was near Detroit.

25. When did the 332nd Fighter Group gain its first black commander, and who was he?

The first black commander of the 332nd Fighter Group was Col. Benjamin O. Davis, Jr., who had commanded the 99th Fighter Squadron in
combat overseas. He took command of the group in October 1943, about
a year after the group was first activated. He took the place of Col. Robert
Selway, a white commander who had also attended West Point. Selway later
commanded the black 477th Bombardment Group.

*Colonel Benjamin O. Davis, Jr., the most famous of all the Tuskegee
Airmen, when he commanded the 332nd Fighter Group in combat.*

26. When did the 332nd Fighter Group deploy overseas?

The 332nd Fighter Group deployed from Michigan to Italy in January 1944.

27. What kinds of missions did the 332nd Fighter Group fly at first?

At first the 332nd Fighter Group flew missions to patrol shipping lanes in the Mediterranean Sea. They later flew in support of ground forces in Italy.

28. What kind of airplanes did the 332nd Fighter Group fly at first in combat?

At first the 332nd Fighter Group flew P-39 airplanes in Italy. Those planes had the engine behind the pilot because the front to that airplane type included a cannon and its ammunition. The P-39 was very good at hitting targets on the ground or sea, but not very good against enemy fighters in air combat.

29. When did the 332nd Fighter Group begin flying bomber escort missions?

The 332nd Fighter Group began flying bomber escort missions in June 1944. It had been transferred from the Twelfth Air Force, which supported surface forces, to the Fifteenth Air Force, which flew heavy bombers escorted by fighters deep into enemy territory.

30. What kinds of airplanes did the 332nd Fighter Group use when it began flying its bomber escort missions?

When it began flying bomber escort missions, the 332nd Fighter Group flew P-47 Thunderbolt airplanes. Sometimes a P-47 was called a Jug. It had a very large air-cooled engine, and was excellent in a dive. Many Tuskegee Airmen liked the airplane because its large engine helped protect them from enemy fire facing them, and because the airplanes were less vulnerable than airplanes with water-cooled engines.

31. What kinds of airplanes did the 332nd Fighter Group escort

on bomber escort missions?

The 332nd Fighter Group escorted heavy bombers such as B-17 Flying Fortresses and the B-24 Liberators. Those four-engine airplanes were comparable in size, but the B-17 could fly higher and was less vulnerable, and the B-24 was a little faster and could fly a little farther. Each heavy bomber had a crew of about 10 men. They also were equipped with machine guns in the nose, in the tail, in a top turret, in a bottom turret, and one on each side. Each bomber had at least ten machine guns and flew in large formations, but they still needed the protection of escort fighters.

32. When was the 99th Fighter Squadron first assigned to the 332nd Fighter Group?

The 99th Fighter Squadron was assigned to the 332nd Fighter Group in May 1944, but did not physically join the group at the same base until July 1944. In the meantime, the 99th Fighter Squadron continued to be

Tuskegee Airmen kneeling in front of a P-51 Mustang, the red-tailed fighter they flew in European combat from July 1944 to April 1945.

attached to other fighter groups.

33. When did the 332nd Fighter Group begin flying P-51 Mustang airplanes in combat?

The 332nd Fighter Group began flying P-51 Mustang airplanes in combat during July 1944.

34. Why were the Tuskegee Airmen pilots, on their bomber escort missions, sometimes called the "Red Tails?"

Each of the four P-51 fighter escort groups in the Fifteenth Air Force had its own identifying color or pattern on the tails of its aircraft. The 31st Fighter Group had striped red tails, the 52nd Fighter Group had solid yellow tails, the, the 325th Fighter Group had black and yellow checkered tails, and the 332nd Fighter Group had solid red tails.

35. What were the two chief advantages of the P-51 Mustang?

The P-51 Mustang could fly faster and farther than other Allied fighters. It was not faster, however than some of the German jets.

36. Where was the 332nd Fighter Group based for its bomber escort missions?

For its bomber escort missions for the Fifteenth Air Force, the 332nd Fighter Group was based at Ramitelli Airfield, which was on the Foggia Plain near the Adriatic Sea, on the east coast of central Italy.

37. What were the two most important differences between the 332nd Fighter Group and the other fighter escort groups in the Fifteenth Air Force?

The 332nd Fighter Group was the only black fighter group, and it was the only one to have four squadrons instead of three. That gave it more pilots and more airplanes than the average fighter group.

38. How did the numbers of fighter escorts compare with the number of bombers they were assigned to escort?

There were always many more bombers to escort than there were fighters to escort them. By the summer of 1944, the Fifteenth Air Force had seven fighter escort groups, all but one of them with three fighter squadrons each. The Fifteenth Air Force at the same time had twenty-one bombardment groups, each group with four bombardment squadrons. For every fighter escort group, there were three bombardment groups. It is no wonder that sometimes bombers under fighter escort group protection would sometimes be shot down by enemy aircraft, because often there were many more bombers than fighters to protect them, and more enemy fighters than fighter escorts to fend them off.

39. Did the Red Tails ever lose a bomber under their protection to enemy airplanes?

On at least seven of the 179 bomber escort missions the 332nd Fighter Group flew for the Fifteenth Air Force, bombers under Tuskegee Airmen escort were shot down by enemy aircraft. A total of at least 27 Tuskegee Airmen-escorted bombers were lost to enemy fighters.

40. How did the 332nd Fighter Group compare with the other fighter groups of the Fifteenth Air Force, in terms of performance?

The 332nd Fighter Group performance compared favorably with the other fighter groups with which it served overseas during World War II. The group lost significantly fewer bombers to enemy airplanes than those other fighter groups in the Fifteenth Air Force. The 332nd Fighter Group lost a total of 27 bombers, but the average number of bombers lost by each of the other fighter groups was 46. In the period between early June 1944 and the end of April 1945, the 332nd Fighter Group was fifth of the seven fighter groups in the number of aerial victories it achieved. The 332nd Fighter Group shot down more enemy fighters in that period than two of the other fighter escort groups, but those other groups were flying P-38 airplanes. During the period between the beginning of June 1944 and the end of April 1945, when it was flying for the Fifteenth Air Force, the 332nd Fighter Group shot down fewer enemy airplanes than the other P-51 fighter groups in the Fifteenth Air Force.

41. How many combat missions did the Tuskegee Airmen fly?

The 99th Fighter Squadron flew 577 missions before joining the 332nd Fighter Group, and the 332nd Fighter Group flew 914 missions, for a total of 1491 combat missions flown by the Tuskegee Airmen.

42. How many combat missions did the 332nd Fighter Group fly for the Fifteenth Air Force?

The 332nd Fighter Group flew a total of 312 combat missions for the Fifteenth Fighter Group between the beginning of June 1944 and the end of April 1945.

43. How many of the 312 combat missions of the 332nd Fighter Group for the Fifteenth Air Force escorted bombers?

The 332nd Fighter Group flew a total of 179 bomber escort missions for the Fifteenth Air Force. 172 of these were heavy bomber escort, or escort for 4-engine bombers such as B-17s or B-24s. The other 7 escorted medium bombers, or twin engine bombers such as B-25s or B-26s. The Tuskegee Airmen had escorted medium bombers before, for the Twelfth Air Force, but bomber escort was not their primary job before they were assigned to the Fifteenth Air Force.

44. Had the 99th Fighter Squadron ever escorted medium bombers that were shot down by enemy aircraft before the 99th Fighter Squadron was assigned to the 332nd Fighter Group?

Yes. The 99th Fighter Squadron escorted medium bombers on July 3, 1943, when it was attached to the 324th Fighter Group, and two of those bombers were shot down by enemy airplanes.

45. What was the most memorable mission of the 332nd Fighter Group?

The most memorable mission of the 332nd Fighter Group was a mission

Many of the Tuskegee Airmen were not pilots but support personnel on the ground, such as these enlisted men equipping a P-51 red-tailed Mustang with fuel tanks.

to escort bombers to Berlin on March 24, 1945. It was the only Fifteenth Air Force mission to the enemy capital, and it was the longest mission flown by the Fifteenth Air Force. During that mission, three Tuskegee airmen each shot down a German Me-262 jet airplane. Other fighter escort groups also flew on that mission, and one of those other fighter groups also shot down German jets. The Berlin mission is the one for which the 332nd Fighter Group earned a Distinguished Unit Citation.

46. What were all the aircraft types the Tuskegee Airmen flew in combat?

The Tuskegee Airmen flew four different kinds of aircraft in combat: P-39s, P-40s, P-47s, and P-51s. The 99th Fighter Squadron at first flew P-40s in North Africa, Sicily, and Italy, in 1943 and 1944. The 332nd Fighter

Group and its 100th, 301st, and 302nd Fighter Squadrons at first flew P-39s and then P-47s in 1944. By the end of July 1944, the 99th Fighter Squadron had joined the 332nd Fighter Group, and all of its squadrons were flying P-51s.

47. How many honors did the 332d Fighter Group earn?

Besides campaign streamers, the 332nd Fighter Group earned one Distinguished Unit Citation, for the Berlin mission.

48. How many honors did the 99th Fighter Squadron earn, before it was assigned to the 332nd Fighter Group?

The 99th Fighter Squadron earned two Distinguished Unit Citations before it was assigned to the 332d Fighter Group. The 99th Fighter Squadron earned a total of three Distinguished Unit Citations, because it earned a third one after being assigned to the 332d Fighter Group.

49. How many enemy airplanes did the Tuskegee Airmen shoot down?

The 99th Fighter Squadron shot down 18 enemy airplanes before it was assigned to the 332nd Fighter Group, and the 332nd Fighter Group and its squadrons shot down 94 enemy airplanes, for a total of 112 enemy airplanes shot down by the Tuskegee Airmen.

50. Were there any Tuskegee Airmen aces?

No. During World War II, none of the Tuskegee Airmen claimed to have shot down any more than four enemy airplanes, and none received any more than four aerial victory credits. However, three Tuskegee Airmen (Lee Archer, Joseph Elsberry, and Edward Toppins) each shot down a total of four enemy airplanes, and four of the Tuskegee Airmen (Joseph Elsberry, Clarence Lester, Lee Archer, and Harry Stewart) each shot down three enemy airplanes in one day. One reason there were no Tuskegee Airmen aces in the 332nd Fighter Group is that it deployed and began flying bomber escort missions later than the other fighter escort groups in the Fifteenth Air Force.

Brig. Gen. Benjamin O. Davis, Sr., the first black general in the U.S. Army, pinning the Distinguished Flying Cross on his son, then Col. Benjamin O. Davis, Jr., who later went on to become the first black general in the U.S. Air Force.

51. Who was the most important leader of the 99th Fighter Squadron and the 332nd Fighter Group?

The most important commander of the 99th Fighter Squadron, and later the 332nd Fighter Group, was Col. Benjamin O. Davis, Jr. He was a West Point graduate whose father was the first black general in the Army. Benjamin O. Davis, Jr. later became the first black general in the Air Force.

52. How many Tuskegee Airmen pilots deployed overseas for combat during World War II?

355 Tuskegee Airmen pilots deployed overseas for combat.

53. How many Tuskegee Airmen pilots who deployed overseas

failed to return?

According to researcher Craig Huntly, 81 Tuskegee Airmen were killed overseas.

54. How many Tuskegee Airmen earned Distinguished Flying Crosses?

95 Tuskegee Airmen earned Distinguished Flying Crosses, but one of them earned two, so the Tuskegee Airmen earned a total of 96 Distinguished Flying Crosses.

55. How many Tuskegee Airmen became prisoners of war after having been shot down over enemy territory?

31 Tuskegee Airmen became prisoners of war after having been shot down over enemy territory.

56. What happened to the 332d Fighter Group after the end of the war in Europe?

The War Department inactivated the 332d Fighter Group temporarily, soon after the war in Europe ended.

57. What black flying organization in the United States trained replacement pilots for the 332nd Fighter Group and its squadrons when they were deployed overseas?

The 553rd Fighter Squadron, which served at Selfridge Field and Oscoda Field in Michigan between 1 November 1943 and 5 May 1944, trained replacement pilots for the 332d Fighter Group and its squadrons deployed overseas. Fighter pilots who graduated from Tuskegee Army Air Field after the deployment of the 332nd Fighter Group were often assigned first to the 553nd Fighter Group, and not directly to the deployed 332nd Fighter Group.

58. What was the first black bombardment group, and when was it first activated as a black flying organization?

The 477th Bombardment Group was the first black bombardment group. It had been active briefly in 1943 as a white bombardment group, but when it was activated again, at Selfridge Field, Michigan, on 15 January 1944, it was a black bombardment group. It received its pilots from twin-engine training at Tuskegee. Between January and May 1944, both the 477th Bombardment Group and the 553rd Fighter Squadron served at Selfridge Field, Michigan.

59. Who was the first commander of the black 477th Bombardment Group?

The first commander of the 477th Bombardment Group, after it was activated as a black bombardment group in January 1944, was Col. Robert Selway, a white officer who had commanded the 332nd Fighter Group at the same base, Selfridge Field, Michigan, before it deployed overseas. Selway remained the commander of the group for a year and a half. He was not popular with the black officers, since he attempted to enforce segregation on the bases where the group was stationed. At Selfridge, he wanted to keep the officers club restricted to whites, but reluctantly agreed that a black officers club could also be established. At Godman Field, Kentucky, blacks used the officers club, but only because the white officers used the officers club at Fort Knox next door. At Freeman Field, Indiana, Selway set up two Officers Clubs, one for whites and one for blacks.

60. What were the squadrons assigned to the 477th Bombardment Group?

The 477th Bombardment Group had four bombardment squadrons, the 616th, 617th, 618th, and 619th.

61. Why did the 477th Bombardment Group never deploy overseas or take part in combat?

The 477th Bombardment Group never deployed overseas for combat partly because it was activated so late in the war (in January 1944); partly because a bombardment group took longer to train than a fighter group; and partly because it was transferred from base to base because of racial trouble.

62. What was the most important event in 477th Bombardment

Group history?

The most important event in 477th Bombardment Group history was later called the "Freeman Field Mutiny," in April 1945. 61 black officers were arrested at first for trying to enter the all-white officers club, but all but 3 of them were released at first. 101 black officers, many of whom were in the original group of 61, were later arrested for refusing to sign a document acknowledging the segregated officers clubs policy. A total of 120 black officers of the 477th Bombardment Group were arrested. They were all later exonerated except for 1 officer, Roger Terry, who was convicted for "jostling." He, too, was eventually exonerated. Most of the black officers of the 477th Bombardment Group signed the document, and were not arrested.

63. How were the racial problems within the 477th Bombardment Group ended?

In the summer of 1945, the Army Air Forces reassigned all the white officers in the 477th Bombardment Group, including its commander, Col. Robert Selway, to other organizations, and replaced them with black officers. Col. Benjamin O. Davis, Jr., returning from Europe after the Allied victory there, became commander of the 477th. The group itself was redesignated as the 477th Composite Group at the same time, because the 99th Fighter Squadron was reassigned to it, and it then had both bombers and fighters.

64. What happened to the 477th Composite Group after that?

The 477th Composite Group remained active for a couple years after the war, and moved during that time to Lockbourne Air Force Base, Ohio. In 1947, it was replaced by the 332nd Fighter Group, which was activated again.

65. What was the final accomplishment of the 332nd Fighter Group before it was inactivated in 1949?

The 332nd Fighter Group won the conventional (propeller) aircraft category at an Air Force gunnery meet in Las Vegas in 1949. Another group won the jet airplane category.

66. How were the armed forces of the United States integrated?

President Truman is usually given credit for mandating the racial integration of the armed forces by issuing Executive Order 9981 in 1948. However, the United States Air Force, which had become independent from the Army in 1947, had already announced that it would racially integrate months before Truman's action, and in 1949, it became the first of the armed services to achieve significant racial integration. On 11 May 1949, the Air Force issued letter 35-3, which prescribed racially integrated United States Air Force organizations. On 1 Jul 1949, the all-black 332nd Fighter Wing and its 332nd Fighter Group were inactivated, and their personnel were reassigned to formerly all-white flying organizations. The Army and the Navy did not achieve racial integration until later.

67. Why did many of the Tuskegee Airmen remain in the Air Force after World War II, and eventually fly in the Korean and Vietnam wars, too?

Many Tuskegee Airmen wanted to remain pilots, but most commercial airline companies would not hire them just after World War II, partly because there were so many white transport pilots returning from war service, who had more experience in airliner-type aircraft. There were no black transport flying units during World War II. In order to keep flying as their vocation, many of the Tuskegee Airmen remained in the Air Force. Of course, many of them enjoyed serving their country, and wanted to remain in the service, despite whatever opportunities there might have been beyond military service.

68. Who were some of the other famous Tuskegee Airmen?

One of the other famous Tuskegee Airmen, besides Benjamin O. Davis, Jr. were Daniel "Chappie" James, who had served in the 477th Bombardment Group, and who later flew fighters in Korea and Vietnam. He became the first black four-star general in any of the military services. Another famous Tuskegee Airman was Col. Charles McGee, who flew fighter airplanes in combat in World War II, Korea, and Vietnam, and who accumulated a total of 409 combat missions, one of the highest totals of any USAF pilot, but not the highest. Still another famous Tuskegee Airman was Roscoe Brown, one of three Tuskegee Airmen to shoot down a German jet. He later earned a doctorate in education. Lt. Col. Lee Archer was also another famous Tuskegee Airman. He shot down four enemy airplanes in World War II. He was not an ace, despite stories that he was, but he became successful as a businessman after World War II. 1st Lt. Charles B. Hall was the first Tuskegee Airman to shoot down an enemy aircraft (on 2 July 1943). 1st Lieutenant George B. Roberts became the first black commander of

Daniel "Chappie" James was a Tuskegee Airman during World War II who later flew in Korea and Vietnam and became the first four-star African American general in U.S. history.

the first black flying unit, the 99th Fighter Squadron, on 1 June 1942. 1st Lt. Joseph D. Elsberry was the first Tuskegee Airman to shoot down three enemy airplanes in one day, on 12 July 1944. Besides Col. Benjamin O. Davis, Jr., Captain Robert B. Tresville was another Tuskegee Airman who was a graduate of the U.S. Military Academy at West Point. He was killed in action on 24 June 1944, while commanding the 100th Fighter Squadron. There are many other Tuskegee Airmen who became well known.

69. What is a DOTA?

A DOTA is a Documented Original Tuskegee Airman. The definition of a Documented Original Tuskegee Airman was drafted by the members of the Tuskegee Airmen Incorporated to help determine which of their members was an original Tuskegee Airman, based on documents supplied by the member. Please see the answer to question 1 for more information.

70. Who invented the term "Tuskegee Airmen"?

The first book written about the Tuskegee Airmen was called THE TUSKEGEE AIRMEN, and it was first published in 1955. The author, Charles Francis, called the first black military pilots Tuskegee Airmen because they had trained at Tuskegee.

71. What was one reason people did not at first know much about the Tuskegee Airmen?

For many years after World War II, the primary sources of Tuskegee Airmen history were, like the histories of white units, classified. Once those documents were declassified, the units became better known.

72. Where are the most important primary sources of the Tuskegee Airmen located?

Most of the primary sources of Tuskegee Airmen unit history are located at the Air Force Historical Research Agency at Maxwell Air Force Base. Those documents include the monthly histories of the various Tuskegee Airmen groups and squadrons written by Tuskegee Airmen during the war, the daily narrative mission reports of the combat organizations, also written by Tuskegee Airmen during the war, orders that awarded the first black military pilots honors such as aerial victory credits and Distinguished Flying Crosses and other awards, reports on missing air crews, escape and evasion reports, and mission folders of the Fifteenth Air Force.

73. What are some of the most common inaccuracies told about the Tuskegee Airmen?

The most common inaccuracies told about the Tuskegee Airmen are that they were the only fighter escort group never to have lost a bomber to enemy aircraft (they actually lost 27); that Lee Archer was the first black ace (there were no Tuskegee Airmen aces during World War II, and Lee Archer earned four aerial victory credits); that the Tuskegee Airmen were the first American pilots to shoot down German jets (many American pilots had shot down German jets before the Tuskegee Airmen did); and that the Tuskegee Airmen sank a German destroyer (the ship they attacked on the day and place in question did not sink, and was not scuttled until the next year).

74. What is the historical significance of the Tuskegee Airmen?

The historical significance of the Tuskegee Airmen is that they were the first black pilots in American military history, and by performing well in combat, proved that they fully deserved the same opportunities offered to white pilots and servicemen. Their record encouraged the Air Force to integrate before the other services. The Tuskegee Airmen provided role models for others, demonstrating how determination and persistence can overcome many obstacles. They risked their lives for their country even at a time when they were denied equal opportunities, and their actions helped open the door of equal opportunity to others of their race.

75. Were the Tuskegee Airmen the only black personnel in the Army Air Forces during World War II?

The Tuskegee Airmen were not the only black personnel in the Army Air Forces during World War II, but they were the only ones flying in combat. Other black organizations in the Army Air Forces during the war included members of a host of engineer aviation battalions, who constructed airfields for the service all over the world, and not just in the Mediterranean Theater.

76. Did any Tuskegee Airmen ever serve in the Pacific Ocean areas during World War II?

The only Tuskegee Airmen who served in the Pacific Ocean area during World War II were some of the liaison pilots who were assigned to Army ground organizations after training at Tuskegee. For example, fourteen of the black liaison pilots of the 93rd Division (also black) trained at Tuskegee, and the 93rd Division served in the South Pacific. None of the fighter or bomber pilots among the Tuskegee Airmen served in the Pacific.

About the Author

DR. DANIEL L. HAULMAN is Chief, Organization History Division, at the Air Force Historical Research Agency, where he has worked since 1982. He earned his Bachelor's degree from the University of Southwestern Louisiana in 1971, his Master's degree from the University of New Orleans in 1975, and his Ph.D. in history from Auburn University in 1983. His dissertation examined the first state constitutions and how they differed from the colonial frames of government. During the 1970s, he worked at Charity Hospital in New Orleans and taught high school social studies in Louisiana for five years. He has authored seven books about aviation history, including *Air Force Aerial Victory Credits: World War I, World War II, Korea, and Vietnam*; *The United States and Air Force and Humanitarian Airlift Operations, 1947-1994*; *One Hundred Years of Flight: USAF Chronology of Significant Air and Space Events, 1903-2002*; *The Tuskegee Airmen: An Illustrated History, 1939-1949* (with Joseph Caver and Jerome Ennels), *Eleven Myths About the Tuskegee Airmen*, *The Tuskegee Airmen and the Never Lost a Bomber Myth*, and *What Hollywood Got Right and Wrong About the Tuskegee Airmen*. Dr. Haulman has also written three Air Force pamphlets, including *The High Road to Tokyo Bay*; *Hitting Home: The Air Offensive Against Japan;* and *Wings of Hope: The U.S. Air Force and Humanitarian Airlift Operations*. He has composed sections of other USAF publications and compiled the list of official USAF aerial victories appearing on the Air Force Historical Research Agency's internet web page. He wrote the Air Force chapter in supplement IV of *A Guide to the Sources of United States Military History* and completed six studies on aspects of recent USAF operations that have been used by the Air Staff and Air University. He has also written two of five chapters in the latest edition of *Locating Air Force Base Sites: History's Legacy,* a book about the location of Air Force bases, and eleven articles in *Short of War*, a book about the United States Air Force in twenty-three contingency operations. The author of more than twenty published articles in various journals, Dr. Haulman has also presented twenty-seven different historical papers at historical conferences and taught ten college courses, one each at Auburn University and Auburn University Montgomery, and four each at Huntingdon College and Faulkner University in Montgomery, Alabama. He is married to Ellen Evans Haulman, and they have a son named Evan.

ALSO BY DANIEL HAULMAN

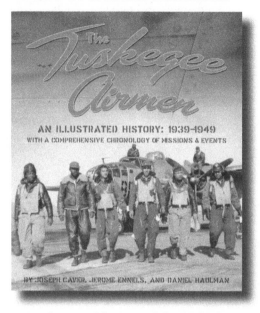

Experience the visual history of the Tuskegee Airmen . . .

Many documentaries, articles, museum exhibits, books, and movies have now treated the subject of the Tuskegee Airmen, the only black American military pilots in World War II. Most of these works have focused on their training and their subsequent accomplishments during combat.

The Tuskegee Airmen: An Illustrated History goes further, using captioned photographs to trace the Airmen through the various stages of training, deployment, and combat in North Africa, Italy, and over occupied Europe. Included for the first time are depictions of the critical support roles of nonflyers: doctors, mechanics, and others, all of whom contributed to the Airmen's success. This volume makes vivid the story of the Tuskegee Airmen and the environments in which they lived, worked, played, fought, and sometimes died.

ISBN 978-1-58838-244-3
Available in hardcover
Visit www.newsouthbooks.com/tuskegeeairmen

ALSO BY DANIEL HAULMAN

Learn more about the Tuskegee Airmen . . .

The members of the 332d Fighter Group and the 99th, 100th, 301st, and 302d Fighter Squadrons during World War II are remembered in part because they were the only African American pilots who served in combat with the Army Air Forces during the war. They are more often called the Tuskegee Airmen since they trained at Tuskegee Army Air Field. In the more than sixty years since World War II, several stories have grown up about the Tuskegee Airmen, some of them true and some of them false. This book focuses on eleven myths about the Tuskegee Airmen, throughly researched and debunked by Air Force historian Daniel Haulman, with copious historical documentation and sources to prove Haulman's research.

ISBN 978-1-60306-147-6
Available in paperback and ebook
Visit www.newsouthbooks.com/elevenmyths

ALSO BY DANIEL HAULMAN

Investigating the "Never Lost a Bomber" myth . . .

During the first sixty years following World War II, a powerful myth grew up claiming that the Tuskegee Airmen, the only black American military pilots in the war, had been the only fighter escort group never to have lost a bomber to enemy aircraft fire. The myth was enshrined in articles, books, museum exhibits, television programs, and films.

This ebook explores how the "never lost a bomber" myth originated and grew, and then refutes it conclusively with careful reference to primary source documents located at the Air Force Historical Research Agency. By piecing together these historical documents, Daniel Haulman not only proves that sometimes bombers under the escort of the Tuskegee Airmen were shot down by enemy aircraft, but when and where those losses occurred, and to which groups they belonged.

ISBN 978-1-60306-105-6
Available as an ebook
Visit www.newsouthbooks.com/bombermyth

ALSO BY DANIEL HAULMAN

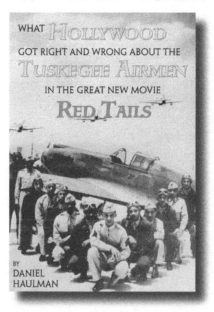

The movie is only the beginning . . .

The new George Lucas movie called *Red Tails* focuses attention on the Tuskegee Airmen of World War II and their combat operations overseas. Loaded with special effects and a great cast, the movie is thrilling and inspiring, but how accurate is it historically? Military historian Daniel Haulman takes an appreciative look at *Red Tails*, comparing it to the actual missions of the Tuskegee Airmen and offering places where interested viewers could study the events further.

"This list of differences between the *Red Tails* depiction of the Tuskegee Airmen and the real Tuskegee Airmen story is not intended to denigrate the movie," Haulman writes in his introduction, "but merely to caution those who might mistakenly take the fictional account as history."

ISBN 978-1-60306-160-5
Available as an ebook
Visit www.newsouthbooks.com/redtails

CPSIA information can be obtained
at www.ICGtesting.com
Printed in the USA
LVHW050716020921
696499LV00004B/14

9 781603 063814